Key Stage 2 English Practice Papers
Contents, Instructions an[...]

Author: Faisal Nasim

Contents

Instructions 2

Answers 3

Set A English Reading Booklet 17

Set B English Reading Booklet 29

Set A

English Reading Paper Answer Booklet 41

English Grammar, Punctuation and Spelling Paper 1: Questions 57

English Grammar, Punctuation and Spelling Paper 2: Spelling 73

Set B

English Reading Paper Answer Booklet 77

English Grammar, Punctuation and Spelling Paper 1: Questions 93

English Grammar, Punctuation and Spelling Paper 2: Spelling 110

Acknowledgements

The author and publisher are grateful to the copyright holders for permission to use quoted materials and images.

Reading booklet Set A: P23 © Douglas Carr/ Alamy Stock Photo; P24 ©Granger Historical Picture Archive/Alamy Stock Photo All other images ©Shutterstock.com

Every effort has been made to trace copyright holders and obtain their permission for the use of copyright material. The author and publisher will gladly receive information enabling them to rectify any error or omission in subsequent editions. All facts are correct at time of going to press.

Published by Collins
An imprint of HarperCollins*Publishers*
1 London Bridge Street
London SE1 9GF

© HarperCollins*Publishers* Limited 2018

ISBN 9780008384500

Content first published 2018
This edition first published 2019

10 9 8 7 6 5 4 3 2 1

British Library Cataloguing in Publication Data.

A CIP record of this book is available from the British Library.

Author: Faisal Nasim
Contributor: Jon Goulding
Commissioning Editors: Michelle I'Anson and Alison James
Editor and Project Manager: Katie Galloway
Cover Design: Amparo Barrera and Sarah Duxbury
Inside Concept Design: Paul Oates
Text Design and Layout: Aptara® Inc
Production: Karen Nulty
Printed in the UK by Martins The Printers

MIX
Paper from
responsible source
FSC www.fsc.org **FSC** C007454

This book is produced from independently certified FSC™ paper to ensure responsible forest management.

For more information visit:
www.harpercollins.co.uk/green

Instructions

Introduction

This practice resource consists of two complete sets of Key Stage 2 English practice test papers. Each set contains similar test papers to those that pupils will take at the end of Year 6:

- **Reading** – each test is made up of three different texts (in a reading booklet), and an answer booklet.
- **Grammar, Punctuation and Spelling** – each test is made up of Paper 1 and Paper 2. Paper 1 contains 50 questions; Paper 2 contains 20 spellings. The spelling test administration guide can be found on pages 9 and 16 of this answers booklet.

These test papers can be used any time throughout the year to provide practice for the Key Stage 2 tests.

Administering the Tests

- Children should work in a quiet environment where they can complete each test undisturbed.
- The amount of time per test varies, so children should check the time given on each test paper.
- Handwriting is not assessed but children should write their answers clearly.

Marking the Tests

Each set of English practice papers contains a Reading paper and two Grammar, punctuation and spelling papers:

- Reading is worth 50 marks
- Grammar, punctuation and spelling Paper 1 is worth 50 marks
- Grammar, punctuation and spelling Paper 2 is worth 20 marks

Total = 70 marks

Use this answer booklet to mark the test papers.

Add up the total marks for the Reading paper. As a general guideline, if a child gets 26 or more marks on the Reading paper (i.e. 28 or more out of 50), they are reaching the expected standard.

Add up the total marks for the Grammar, punctuation and spelling Paper 1 and Grammar, punctuation and spelling Paper 2. As a general guideline, if a child gets 38 or more marks across the two papers (i.e. 38 or more out of 70), they are reaching the expected standard.

Keep in mind that the exact number of marks required to achieve the expected standard may vary year by year depending on the overall difficulty of the test.

Answers

Set A Reading

Content domain coverage for the questions in this paper are shown in the table of answers below. Information about these codes can be found in the KS2 English Reading test framework.

Question (Content domain)		Requirement	Mark
1	(2d)	Award 1 mark for **It is raining.**	1
2	(2a)	Award 1 mark for **indulged**	1
3	(2b)	Award 1 mark for reference to any of the following: • Peter hasn't got any Pickeez. • Peter isn't getting the new toys at the same time as his friends. • Peter's mother sometimes tells him 'no'. • Peter has asked for a new toy but hasn't received it. Do not accept any reference to the weather, Peter's boring day or his having to walk through puddles.	1
4	(2d)	Award 1 mark for a reference to Peter being in a bad mood or specifically a bad mood with his mother or that he wanted her to feel guilty, e.g. • Peter was cross because he couldn't have the Pickeez. • Peter was mad at his mum. • Peter wanted the toys and was angry that his mum said no. • Peter wanted his mum to feel guilty for not buying him the toy. Do not accept 'He was sent to his room'.	1
5	(2b)	Accept any reference to the following two obsessions listed in the text: • plastic spinners • football cards Do not accept general references to 'toys' or 'games'.	1
6	(2a)	Award 1 mark for reference to any of the following: • Nobody was really speaking to each other. • Everyone was cross so nobody spoke. • The mealtime was less lively than usual. • They would normally chat but today they didn't. Accept any other reference to the contrast between a normal mealtime and the more subdued version in the story, e.g. they weren't as happy as they usually are.	1
7	(2a)	Award 1 mark for a reference to any of the following: • The toys were thrown across the floor. • The toys hadn't been tidied away. • Peter didn't look after his toys very well. • The toys were just left where they'd been dropped. • There were a lot of toys in the room. • Peter had moved on to new things and left the old toys out. • Peter didn't appreciate the things he had. Do not accept reference to Peter throwing the toys down in anger, e.g. Peter threw the toys down because he couldn't have what he wanted.	1
8	(2b)	Award 1 mark for references to Peter feeling ashamed (for not remembering the boy's name). Do not accept references to Peter feeling dejected or full of self-pity.	1
9	(2d)	Award 1 mark for one of the following with a plausible justification. Award 2 marks for two of the following with plausible justifications. • It says 'she sighed', which indicates she felt fed-up/exasperated/sad/disappointed as he already had lots of toys. • She says, 'Oh Peter, if only you'd…', which suggests she is annoyed that he can't see sense/see her viewpoint. • The text says that she 'cleared the dishes in silence', which suggests she is angry and/or reflecting on Peter's behaviour.	Up to 2
10	(2a)	Award 1 mark for **Peter was seeing someone else's point of view for once.**	1
11	(2d)	Award 1 mark for what Peter will say and 1 mark for the reason, e.g. • Peter will apologise to his mum because he feels guilty for how he behaved. • Peter will say sorry to his mum for acting spoilt/being rude.	2
12	(2b)	Award 1 mark for any reference to Peter's mother, e.g. • Mum	1

Question (Content domain)		Requirement	Mark
13	(2d)	Both parts of the question need answering for 2 marks. 0 marks for a partly answered question. The answer must include that Peter realised how lucky/fortunate he was and that he will change by being more grateful for what he has got/not constantly asking for new things.	Up to 2
14	(2a)	Award 1 mark for both of the following: • (the) trend • fashionable (contrast) Do not accept 'popular'.	1
15	(2b)	Award 1 mark for reference to the First World War, e.g. 'The poor times during the war' or 'The wartime'.	1
16	(2a)	Award 1 mark for **high-tech**	1
17	(2b)	Award 1 mark for all four correct: Bellbottomed trousers were originally designed for the army. (FALSE) Frisbees are usually 20–25 cm in diameter. (TRUE) Cabbage Patch Kids were invented in the 1890s. (FALSE) The Frisbee craze hit the United States in the 1950s. (TRUE)	1
18	(2b)	Award 1 mark for each of the following up to a maximum of 2 marks: • Bellbottoms weren't available everywhere – people made their own. • Cabbage Patch Kids were in high demand – shops held lotteries to allocate the dolls. Accept any other reasonable explanation of a downside to a craze, along with an acceptable explanation of how it was dealt with or resolved.	Up to 2
19	(2b)	Award 1 mark for each of the following: • individual name • birth certificate	Up to 2
20	(2a)	Award 1 mark for **sky-rocketed**	1
21	(2b)	Award 1 mark for **1948**	1
22	(2b)	Award 1 mark for **USA** Also accept 'America'.	1
23	(2d)	Award 1 mark for **hysteria** Do not accept 'famous'.	1
24	(2b)	Award 1 mark for **49 days** Do not accept '49' without 'days'.	1
25	(2d)	Award 1 mark for all four correct: Kelly's first attempt lasted 13 hours and 13 minutes. (FACT) Alvin Kelly only did reckless things in his lifetime. (OPINION) 20,000 people watched Kelly in Atlantic City. (FACT) Flagpole sitting was the most unusual fad of the 20th century. (OPINION)	1
26	(2c)	Award 1 mark for **A brief history of crazes and fads through the decades.**	1
27	(2f)	Award 1 mark for all correctly matched: Toys – Details about some popular and successful playthings Fashion – The history and beginnings of fashions in clothing Just Crazy! – A description of one of the more unusual crazes from the past Fads, Crazes and Trends over Time – An overview and introduction	1
28	(2d)	Award 1 mark for reference to learning or improving knowledge of science. Do not accept references to being able to make money from selling the slime or it being fun to play with.	1
29	(2d)	Acceptable points: • It can be made using simple ingredients. • It's fun to play with. • It can be personalised. • There are opportunities in the commercial slime business. • It can help with concentration levels in class. • It's doing something creative. Award 2 marks for two acceptable points, with only one supported with evidence. Award 3 marks for two acceptable points, each supported with evidence, e.g. • 'You don't need any special ingredients to make it and if you made a lot of really good slime, you could sell it to your friends to make some money' • 'You could make it with your friends and have a party. It's good to make something fun and not spend all day looking at your phone' Award 2 marks for either two acceptable points, or one acceptable point supported with evidence, e.g. • 'It's fun because lots of people want to try it out' Award 1 mark for two acceptable points or one point supported by evidence, e.g. • 'You can put your own stuff in it'	Up to 3

Question (Content domain)		Requirement	Mark
30a	(2d)	Award 1 mark for any reference to her having made it before, or experimented with the ingredients, e.g. 'She has obviously made lots of different versions, some have worked out and some haven't' or 'She knows what she's talking about because she knows how to make all the different varieties'.	1
30b	(2d)	Award 1 mark for any of the following: • The mess she makes when she makes the slime • The use of the ingredients she needs • The amount of time she is spending Also accept quotations which make an acceptable point. Do not accept references to other people not liking the slime/it creating a problem at school/her selling the slime.	1
31	(2d)	Acceptable points: • Intelligent • Shrewd/astute • Business-like/money-orientated • Manipulative/cunning • Creative Award 2 marks for two acceptable points, with only one supported with evidence. Award 3 marks for two acceptable points, each supported with evidence, e.g. • 'She sort of tricks her friends into wanting the slime she has made by cleverly lending it to them so they want some of their own' • 'She makes people want what she's selling so she can make money' Award 2 marks for either two acceptable points, or one acceptable point with evidence, e.g. • 'She's good at selling her slime. She makes it herself' • 'She makes lots of the slime herself, and it was her idea to sell it' Award 1 mark for two acceptable points or one acceptable point supported with evidence, e.g. • 'She thought selling it would be a good idea' • 'She's clever' Do not accept general responses about Matilda being nice/a good friend, etc.	Up to 3
32	(2d)	Award 1 mark for any two of the following: • astutely • spotted a gap in the market • marketing ploy • maximise sales • 'try before they buy'	1
33	(2d)	Award 1 mark for **At first she loved the idea, but then it became an issue.**	1
34	(2b)	Award 1 mark for reference to both things, and 1 mark for the reason: • Amanda must clean the table and floors because they often have slime on them.	Up to 2
35	(2g)	Award 1 mark for reference to either of the following: • People will be fanatical about it. • Everyone will want it. or • It is aimed at children. • Adults are getting fed up of crazes. or • It's one craze amongst many. • It's another craze to follow others.	1
36	(2d)	Award 1 mark for **safe to use.**	1
37	(2a)	Award 1 mark for: Ready-made slime **makers**	1
		Award 1 mark for: are scrambling to be the **most visible**	1
38	(2b)	Award 1 mark for all four correct: Slime can be made from glue. (TRUE) Borax is also known as sodium borate. (TRUE) Adults are all opposed to slime. (FALSE) Slime can be personalised. (TRUE)	1

Set A English grammar, punctuation and spelling – Paper 1: questions

Content domain coverage for the questions in this paper are shown in the table of answers below. Information about these codes can be found in the KS2 English Grammar, Punctuation and Spelling test framework.

Question (Content domain)	Requirement	Mark
1 (G6.3)	Award 1 mark for all three correct. <table><tr><th>Word</th><th>Suffix</th></tr><tr><td>fear</td><td>able</td></tr><tr><td>read</td><td>ly</td></tr><tr><td>slow</td><td>less</td></tr></table>	1
2 (G1.8)	Award 1 mark for all three correct. <table><tr><th>Sentence</th><th>Determiner</th></tr><tr><td>At the supermarket, I bought _____ peaches.</td><td>the</td></tr><tr><td>I also bought _____ avocado.</td><td>some</td></tr><tr><td>I carried all _____ shopping home.</td><td>an</td></tr></table>	1
3 (G1.9)	Award 1 mark for the correct word circled. My mother brought a (snack) for me after school. or My mother brought (a snack) for me after school.	1
4 (G3.3)	Award 1 mark for three conjunctions inserted correctly. We should bring coats **and** umbrellas **if** the weather looks poor, **but** we should also bring sun cream just in case!	1
5 (G5.3)	Award 1 mark for **Shall I play with Jake today**	1
6 (G1.6)	Award 1 mark for the correct insertion of an appropriate adverb, e.g. He slammed the car door **angrily**. He slammed the car door **hurriedly**. He slammed the car door **quickly**. He slammed the car door **hastily**. Do not accept misspellings of the adverb.	1
7 (G5.10)	Award 1 mark for **I needed several ingredients: some flour, two eggs, sugar and a vanilla pod.**	1
8 (G5.7)	Award 1 mark for all four inverted commas in the correct place: 'When we have finished our writing,' said the teacher, 'we will start a new topic.'	1
9 (G5.6b)	Award 1 mark for a correctly placed comma. Glancing behind her**,** the girl continued down the street.	1
10 (G1.5)	Award 1 mark for the correct pronouns: When the children had finished playing, **they** tidied away all the toys. Dad was so impressed with the tidy room, **he** gave all the children a treat.	1
11 (G4.1d)	Award 1 mark for a correctly completed table. <table><tr><th>Sentence</th><th>Present progressive</th><th>Past progressive</th></tr><tr><td>Sara is getting excited about the birthday party.</td><td>✓</td><td></td></tr><tr><td>Sara was talking about which present to choose.</td><td></td><td>✓</td></tr><tr><td>Sara is preparing a surprise for her friend.</td><td>✓</td><td></td></tr></table>	1
12 (G5.13)	Award 1 mark for **The kind-hearted girl raised money for charity.**	1
13 (G4.1c)	Award 1 mark for **I won't be available to help.**	1
14 (G2.1)	Award 1 mark for all four correct. <table><tr><th>Sentence</th><th>Function</th></tr><tr><td>What a coincidence it was</td><td>question</td></tr><tr><td>Did you enjoy the trip to the theatre</td><td>command</td></tr><tr><td>There were 20 people at the park</td><td>exclamation</td></tr><tr><td>Put the bags down and come inside</td><td>statement</td></tr></table>	1

Question (Content domain)	Requirement	Mark
15 (G7.1)	Award 1 mark for **I travelled to France to visit my sister.**	1
16 (G5.8)	Award 1 mark for the correct expanded form inserted into each box. **She will** call round when **we have** eaten dinner. I **do not** know why.	1
17 (G5.9)	a) Award 1 mark for the correct response. Brackets / a pair of brackets	1
	b) Award 1 mark for the correct response. Commas / a pair of commas or Dashes / a pair of dashes	1
18 (G5.4)	Award 1 mark for two correct sentences ticked. The sentence should end with a full stop instead of an exclamation mark. There should be a question mark after the word pencil.	1
19 (G5.1)	Award 1 mark for **In April, my cousin will fly from London to Rome for a holiday.**	1
20 (G5.11)	Award 1 mark for semi-colon in correct place: My friends are going shopping**;** they need new uniform for school.	1
21 (G5.8)	Award 1 mark for word correctly circled: I can't seem to find (Claire's) phone number and I'm supposed to call her later on.	1
22 (G6.4)	Award 1 mark for **small**	1
23 (G5.5)	Award 1 mark for a correctly completed table.	1

Sentence	Commas used correctly	Commas used incorrectly
We should buy some cheese, bread and a box of eggs.	✓	
They ran all, over the field looking for their lost dog.		✓
My wallet, old and worn, is never very full of money.	✓	
She looked at the clock and, realised she was late.		✓

Question (Content domain)	Requirement	Mark
24 (G1.7)	Award 1 mark for both words circled. They ran (under) the bridge and hid (behind) a large bush.	1
25 (G2.2)	Award 1 mark for the correct response. Was he talking to the police?	1
26 (G4.2)	Award 1 mark for both words circled. He (bit) into his sandwich just as the train (came) into the station.	1
27 (G3.4)	Award 1 mark for an understanding that the subordinate clause has the purpose of explaining why Sam would not go into the water.	1
28 (G1.4)	Award 1 mark for both words circled. Put the kitten down (before) you drop her. I hung out all the washing, (although) the rain clouds were darkening.	1
29 (G3.1)	Award 1 mark for a correctly completed table.	1

	Main clause	Subordinate clause
The light was fading <u>because it was nearly evening time</u>.		✓
The kettle, <u>which was brand new</u>, began to boil.		✓
When the clock struck twelve, <u>my tummy began to rumble</u>.	✓	

Question (Content domain)	Requirement	Mark
30 (G5.6a)	a) Award 1 mark for a correctly placed comma. Once they had asked Mum, Joe and Kate went bowling.	1
	b) Award 1 mark for correctly placed commas. Once they had asked, Mum, Joe and Kate went bowling. Do not accept the use of a serial comma. Once they had asked, Mum, Joe, and Kate went bowling.	1

Question (Content domain)	Requirement	Mark
31 *(G1.4)*	Award 1 mark for both words circled. The puppy wagged his tail furiously, (but) Jack took no notice (and) went inside the house.	1
32 *(G6.2)*	Award 1 mark for an explanation of both sentences, e.g. The customer complained that the chicken was uncooked. *This means that the chicken was raw.* *This means that the chicken was not cooked at all.* The customer complained that the chicken was overcooked. *This means that the chicken has been cooked for too long.*	1
33 *(G1.5a)*	Award 1 mark for the correct possessive pronoun inserted into each sentence. That doll belongs to my sister. The doll is **hers**. The car belongs to them. The car is **theirs**. The keys belong to us. They keys are **ours**. Do not accept a misspelling of the word 'theirs'.	1
34 *(G6.1)*	a) Award 1 mark for a correct explanation of the word synonym, e.g. They are words that have the same meaning.	1

	b) Award 1 mark for a word that is a synonym of the word frightened, e.g.
	   • terrified
	   • scared
		1

35 *(G4.1a)*	Award 1 mark for all three correct. Last Tuesday, the family **went** out for a walk. They **walked** through some woods and **saw** lots of wildlife. Do not accept misspellings of verb forms.	1
36 *(G1.3)*	Award 1 mark for two correct adjectives derived from the given nouns, e.g. Even though she felt **nervous**, Chloe reached out to touch the unicorn's **beautiful** mane. It was a **magical** experience. Do not accept misspellings of the adjectives.	1
37 *(G1.5b)*	Award 1 mark for **who's**	1
38 *(G1.2)*	Award 1 mark for a grammatically correct sentence that uses wish as a verb and that is correctly punctuated, e.g. I wish I could have a pony of my own. Do not accept responses that use an inflected ending of wish, e.g. Sara wished she had more friends.	1
(G1.1)	Award 1 mark for a grammatically correct sentence that uses wish as a noun and that is correctly punctuated, e.g. I made a wish as I blew out the candle. Do not accept responses that use an inflected ending of wish, e.g. The children signed the card with best wishes.	1
39 *(G3.1a)*	Award 1 mark for the full relative clause underlined. The new car <u>which is parked on our driveway</u> is in need of a wash.	1
40 *(G4.4)*	Award 1 mark for a correctly completed table.	1

Sentence	Active	Passive
The chocolate bar was melted by the sun.		✓
The children washed the windows.	✓	
The candles were blown out by the boy.		✓

Question (Content domain)	Requirement	Mark
41 *(G1.6)*	Award 1 mark for both words circled. The children were playing (noisily,) so I had to step (outside.)	1
42 *(G4.4)*	Award 1 mark for a correctly punctuated sentence using the active voice. *The judge sentenced the prisoner.*	1
43 *(G3.2)*	Award 1 mark for **as an expanded noun phrase**	1
44 *(G4.3)*	Award 1 mark for **were**	1
45 *(G4.1b)*	Award 1 mark for an indication that the present perfect form uses the words 'has finished' to show that now the homework is complete.	1
46 *(G5.4)*	Award 1 mark for an indication that the full stop can be replaced with an exclamation mark. '!'	1

Set A English grammar, punctuation and spelling – Paper 2: spelling

1. The word is **misunderstanding**.
There has been some kind of
misunderstanding.
The word is **misunderstanding**.

2. The word is **known**.
I have *known* my best friend for many years.
The word is **known**.

3. The word is **recorded**.
He secretly *recorded* the conversation.
The word is **recorded**.

4. The word is **sensible**.
Sam is the most *sensible* person I know.
The word is **sensible**.

5. The word is **preferred**.
He *preferred* fruit to vegetables.
The word is **preferred**.

6. The word is **conclusion**.
I came to a startling *conclusion*.
The word is **conclusion**.

7. The word is **undervalued**.
I fear the house has been *undervalued*.
The word is **undervalued**.

8. The word is **difference**.
There is a huge *difference* in clothes sizes.
The word is **difference**.

9. The word is **currency**.
We must remember to buy *currency* for
the holiday.
The word is **currency**.

10. The word is **though**.
Even *though* I was afraid, I stood up
to speak.
The word is **though**.

11. The word is **quay**.
The ships were docked at the *quay*.
The word is **quay**.

12. The word is **devious**.
The *devious* king was not popular among his
subjects.
The word is **devious**.

13. The word is **religious**.
Most children have *religious* education
at school.
The word is **religious**.

14. The word is **magician**.
The *magician* captivated the young children.
The word is **magician**.

15. The word is **torrential**.
The *torrential* rain lasted for several hours.
The word is **torrential**.

16. The word is **weightlessness**.
Astronauts experience *weightlessness*
in space.
The word is **weightlessness**.

17. The word is **forgetting**.
I keep *forgetting* where I've put my keys.
The word is **forgetting**.

18. The word is **receipt**.
Keep the *receipt* in case you need to return it.
The word is **receipt**.

19. The word is **competition**.
I won a prize in the *competition*.
The word is **competition**.

20. The word is **viciously**.
The dog *viciously* attacked the new toy.
The word is **viciously**.

Set B Reading

Content domain coverage for the questions in this paper are shown in the table of answers below. Information about these codes can be found in the KS2 English Reading test framework.

Question (Content domain)		Requirement	Mark
1	(2a)	Award 1 mark for **boulders** Do not accept stone.	1
2	(2a)	Award 1 mark for **impressive**	1
3	(2g)	Award 1 mark for reference to any of the following, up to a maximum of 2 marks: • The lakes looked like they were dug out of the ground. • The rivers were quiet/slow and gentle. • The rivers wound around.	Up to 2
4	(2b)	Award 1 mark for recognition that Finn realises Benandonner was much bigger than he had realised e.g. *Benandonner was a great deal bigger than he had previously thought* Also accept reference to Finn's response to seeing the giant, e.g. • Recognition that Finn is in a hurry to get away: *he quickly scrambled home* • Recognition that Finn realises he's made a mistake: *he'd stupidly challenged Benandonner to a fight but realised he probably shouldn't have*	1
5	(2d)	Two separate things must be identified to gain the available mark. These should include the following: • Quickly scrambling home when he realised that Benandonner was bigger than him. (This answer point must include **scrambling home,** not just the realisation of the size difference.) • Finn beginning to shake when Benandonner knocked on his door.	1
6	(2d)	Award 1 mark for reference to any two of the following: • brave • intelligent • quick-thinking • smarter than the giant • inventive Do not accept inaccurate conceptions, e.g. she is a mother.	1
7	(2b)	Award 1 mark for reference to any of the following (whether given as acceptable point or quotation), up to a maximum of 3 marks: • showed him a tree and said it was a spear • showed him a block of wood and said it was a shield • cooked him cake with stones in • pretended Finn was the baby • gave him a drink which made him confused • showed him boulders Finn used to 'play catch' Accept quotations that meet an acceptable point. Longer quotations that cover more than one acceptable point should be awarded 1 mark.	Up to 3
8	(2b)	Award 1 mark for **Overconfident**	1
9a	(2b)	Accept one mark for any of the following: • He struggled to lift the boulder. • He couldn't play with the boulders like Finn.	1
9b	(2b)	Award 1 mark for references to either his only hurting himself a little or that he had good sense, e.g. 'he hurt himself a little' 'luckily he was a tough giant'	1
10	(2b)	Award 1 mark for **The Isle of Man**	1
11	(2b)	Award 1 mark for three correct. Award 2 marks for all four correct: Finn felt great affection for the Scottish giant. (FALSE) Finn built the causeway to make friends with the Scottish giant. (FALSE) Finn was married. (TRUE) Finn underestimated the size of the Scottish giant. (TRUE)	Up to 2
12a	(2b)	Award 1 mark for **summer**.	1
12b	(2b)	Award 1 mark for **fighting with another boy.**	1
12c	(2b)	Award 1 mark for **told them off, gave them a clip around the ear and sent them to bed.**	1
12d	(2b)	Award 1 mark for **bravely checked the chest of drawers.**	1

Question (Content domain)		Requirement	Mark
24	(2d)	Award 1 mark for answers referring to either the relatively cheap cost of the ticket or the smaller amount of space required for third class accommodation compared to other classes, e.g. • It was a cheap ticket to get them across the world. • Third class rooms were smaller so there was space for more of them. Also accept answers which refer to a new start in life, or the chance to sail on a big, new ship. Do not accept answers which refer to there being more third class tickets than any other kind.	1
25	(2d)	Award 1 mark for reference to any of the following: • The ship was bigger than they may have imagined. • The ship was more luxurious than they perhaps expected. • Their second class rooms were like first class on any other ship. Do not accept reference to their having to do less work because of the staff or crew on board the ship.	1
26	(2a)	Award 1 mark for any of: • not completely without hindrance • hindrance • a small coal fire in a bunker • near collision • a bad omen	1
27a	(2b)	Award 1 mark for reference to two of the following: • Some feared the hull was simply too big. • There was a small fire on board before she sailed. • There was a near miss with another ship as *Titanic* left the dock.	1
27b	(2b)	Award 1 mark for both of the following correctly identified: • called for help • ordered the lifeboats to be filled and lowered.	1
28	(2a)	Award 1 mark for **disorganised**	1
29	(2a)	Award 1 mark for reference to any of the following: • She begged them to help the others. • She was pleading for them to turn around. • She was trying not to demand it but really wanted it to happen. Also accept reference to how Molly may have been feeling about those left behind, e.g. Molly may have had family left behind.	1
30	(2b)	Award 1 mark for **John Jacob Astor IV**	1
31	(2a)	Award 1 mark for references which include any of the following: • avoided • went around • tried to miss	1
32	(2a)	Award 1 mark for **unable to conquer the elements**	1
33	(2c)	Award 1 mark for the correct sequence: The aftermath **6** Opposition and rivalry **1** Construction commences **2** Alarm bells and damages **4** Sinking of the ship **3** Chaotic evacuation **5**	1

Set B English grammar, punctuation and spelling – Paper 1: questions

Content domain coverage for the questions in this paper are shown in the table of answers below. Information about these codes can be found in the KS2 English Grammar, Punctuation and Spelling test framework.

Question (Content domain)	Requirement	Mark
1 (G2.2)	Award 1 mark for **At what point did you give up**	1
2 (G5.11)	Award 1 mark for a correctly placed semi-colon: Go and visit your grandmother**;** she is expecting you.	1
3 (G1.5)	Award 1 mark for an indication that the use of the pronoun ('he') avoids repetition of the name 'Harry'.	1
4 (G6.2)	Award 1 mark for **To force out of position.**	1
5 (G4.1b)	Award 1 mark for **was washing**	1
6 (G7.1)	Award 1 mark for the correct words circled. The streamers and balloons (was/⬭were⬭) very brightly-coloured. The first time I saw tigers and lions (⬭was⬭/were) at the zoo. My cousins (was/⬭were⬭) excited about visiting in the holidays.	1
7 (G5.6b)	Award 1 mark for **Without hesitation, Miles accepted the offer of a place at the university.**	1
8 (G5.5)	Award 1 mark for **Noah brushed his teeth, put on his pyjamas, turned out his lamp and went to sleep.**	1
9 (G1.6)	Award 1 mark for **adverb**	1
10 (G5.10)	Award 1 mark for colon in correct place: I have four best friends**:** Tom (my brother), Sam, James and Nathan.	1
11 (G1.8)	Award 1 mark for **determiners**	1
12 (G5.12)	Award 1 mark for **I love going swimming – it's a great way to keep fit.**	1
13 (G1.3)	Award 1 mark for **Ben had a firm grip on the trophy.**	1
14 (G5.9)	Award 1 mark for **The flask holds 1 litre (1000 millilitres) of liquid.**	1
15 (G1.6)	Award 1 mark for an explanation that indicates an understanding that an adverb modifies (accept 'changes') a verb (also accept adjective or adverb if they are in addition to the word 'verb').	1
16 (G1.4)	Award 1 mark for the correct insertion of an appropriate subordinating conjunction, e.g. We stopped off for a drink **because** it was a hot day. We stopped off for a drink **as** it was a hot day. We stopped off for a drink **since** it was a hot day.	1
17 (G2.4)	Award 1 mark for **What a lot of pizza you have eaten**	1
18 (G1.2)	Award 1 mark for **I began to chip at the dried plaster.**	1
19 (G1.7)	Award 1 mark for the inclusion of a preposition indicating an understanding of this type of word to express *when* the child was looking carefully, e.g. *before* or *while* crossing the road.	1
20 (G1.5)	Award 1 mark for correctly placed pronouns: Sarah asked her parents for some pocket money but **they** asked **her** to clean out the rabbit hutch first.	1
21 (G5.7)	Award 1 mark for **The teacher asked, "Who owns this bag?"**	1
22 (G7.3)	Award 1 mark for **You are cordially invited to a party.**	1
23 (G3.4)	Award 1 mark for **The class, <u>which is mainly boys</u>, loves science lessons.**	1
24 (G6.1)	Award 1 mark for correct circling. Despite the twins appearing to be ⬭identical⬭ they are actually ⬭different⬭ in many ways.	1
25 (G5.8)	Award 1 mark for a correctly completed table.	1

	Apostrophe for omission	Apostrophe for possession
My mother's friend is called Tina.		✓
We're going away tomorrow.	✓	
The dog's collar is broken.		✓
She's bringing some cakes tomorrow.	✓	

Question (Content domain)	Requirement	Mark
26 (G3.1a)	Award 1 mark for **A girl who I know from school is coming to karate class.**	1
27 (G2.1)	Award 1 mark for **I will pack a picnic for everyone to share**	1
28 (G5.2)	Award 1 mark for capital letters and full stops correctly inserted. Jane picked up the full rubbish bag**.** **S**he carried it to the bin**.** **S**he opened the lid but an enormous split appeared in the bag**.** **T**here was rubbish all over the floor**.**	1
29 (G5.6a)	Award 1 mark for a correctly placed pair of commas. The team**,** which was made up of children at my school**,** won the match easily.	1
30 (G4.2)	Award 1 mark for any correct choice of tense for both verbs. For example, The mice **nibbled** at the corner of the box of cat food. Josh **spoke** very softly when he gave his reasons for leaving.	1
31 (G2.3)	Award 1 mark for a grammatically correct and accurately punctuated command that uses an imperative, e.g. *Put toothpaste on the brush.* *Take out your toothbrush.* *Brush your teeth!*	1
32 (G3.1)	Award 1 mark for all three correct. As the book was so interesting (S), I found myself reading it often (M) and offered to share it with the class (M).	1
33 (G1.4)	Award 1 mark for all three correct. They bought new running shoes (when) the sale was on. (Although) the weather was poor, they were determined to cross the finish line. The race went extremely well, (so) they decided to sign up for another.	1
34 (G1.7)	Award 1 mark for both: **The tortoise moved very slowly towards the lettuce.** **My cat walked carefully along the garden fence.**	1
35 (G1.9)	Award 1 mark for John	1
36 (G1.4)	Award 1 mark for a grammatically correct sentence, which includes a conjunction indicating an understanding of this type of word to express cause, such as 'because', 'so', e.g. I am hungry **because** I forgot to have breakfast. She was late **so** she missed the bus.	1
37 (G1.5b)	Award 1 mark for the correct word circled. My mother sent me an enormous fruit basket, (which) contained bananas, grapes, cherries and a mango.	1
38 (G4.1a)	Award 1 mark for all three correct. I **took** my car to a mechanic yesterday to have it **repaired** but I **was** not prepared for the cost! Do not accept misspellings of verb forms.	1
39 (G5.9)	Award 1 mark for a correctly placed pair of brackets The most populated city in the world is Tokyo **(**population 37,833,000**)** in Japan.	1
40 (G6.2) (G6.1)	Award 1 mark for the correct prefix: un	1
41 (G6.1)	Award 1 mark for both synonyms circled. The (stories) written by Roald Dahl are popular with children and adults around the world. His (tales) are captivating and yet sometimes a little dark.	1
42 (G1.5a)	Award 1 mark for the correct word circled. I was completely surprised that Sam didn't only eat Amara's ice cream but ate (yours) as well.	1
43 (G5.11)	Award 1 mark for **semi-colon**	1
44 (G6.3)	Award 1 mark for two correct words derived from the word care, e.g. He **carelessly** dropped litter all over the park. He was always **caring** for stray animals he found in the village. Do not accept misspellings.	1
45 (G1.1)	Award 1 mark for the correct noun inserted. She always found badminton to be a source of great **enjoyment**. Do not accept misspellings of enjoyment.	1
46 (G5.13)	Award 1 mark for two correctly placed hyphens. On the way home, I could tell the children were **over-tired**, which they demonstrated in a very **bad-tempered** way.	1

Question (Content domain)	Requirement	Mark
47 *(G4.4)*	Award 1 mark for a correctly punctuated sentence using the active. The babysitter put the exhausted children to bed.	1
48 *(G4.1d)*	Award 1 mark for both correct. Judy **is baking** cakes. She **is hoping** to sell them to her friends on Monday. Do not accept misspellings of verb forms.	1
49 *(G3.2)*	Award 1 mark for an appropriate noun phrase of three or more words inserted into the sentence, e.g. The landscape gardener was working hard in the garden. My wonderful father was working hard in the garden. The young boy was working hard in the garden.	1
50 *(G1.6)*	Award 1 mark for the correct word circled. You should think ⟨hard⟩ about your options before making such an untimely intervention.	1

Set B English grammar, punctuation and spelling – Paper 2: spelling

Instructions

Read the following instruction out to the child(ren).

I am going to read 20 sentences to you. Each sentence has a word missing. Listen carefully to the missing word and fill this in the answer space, making sure that you spell it correctly. I will read the word, then the word within a sentence, then repeat the word a third time.

You should now read the spellings three times, as given below. Leave at least a 12-second gap between spellings. At the end, read all the sentences again, giving the child(ren) the chance to make any changes they wish to their answers.

1. The word is **happily**.
They played *happily* together for hours.
The word is **happily**.

2. The word is **caught**.
I *caught* a cold that lasted for a week.
The word is **caught**.

3. The word is **nation**.
Trade with other countries brings jobs and wealth to our *nation*.
The word is **nation**.

4. The word is **obvious**.
It is *obvious* to me when you are lying.
The word is **obvious**.

5. The word is **design**.
She put a great deal of work into her *design*.
The word is **design**.

6. The word is **incredible**.
They found the stories of her adventures quite *incredible*.
The word is **incredible**.

7. The word is **confusing**.
The new way of organising the paperwork is quite *confusing*.
The word is **confusing**.

8. The word is **emergency**.
I know how to dial 999 in the event of an *emergency*.
The word is **emergency**.

9. The word is **compassion**.
He demonstrated real *compassion* for the refugees.
The word is **compassion**.

10. The word is **roughest**.
The sailor looked out at the *roughest* sea he had ever encountered.
The word is **roughest**.

11. The word is **thistle**.
Things were going well until she was scratched by a *thistle* in the grass.
The word is **thistle**.

12. The word is **probably**.
This is *probably* the longest I have ever spent at my desk.
The word is **probably**.

13. The word is **vacancy**.
The hotel manager advertised a *vacancy* for a receptionist.
The word is **vacancy**.

14. The word is **understanding**.
He was a very *understanding* and patient parent.
The word is **understanding**.

15. The word is **troubling**.
Something is *troubling* him, but I'm not sure what it is.
The word is **troubling**.

16. The word is **chemist**.
I must pop into the *chemist* for cough medicine on the way home.
The word is **chemist**.

17. The word is **myths**.
My favourite stories are *myths* and legends.
The word is **myths**.

18. The word is **amazingly**.
Amazingly, everyone got on with each other all day.
The word is **amazingly**.

19. The word is **solution**.
The boys worked all morning on a *solution* to the maths problem.
The word is **solution**.

20. The word is **cheque**.
Grandma said she is sending me a *cheque* for my birthday.
The word is **cheque**.

All the Wonderful Things

Mad Fad Memorabilia

Put the Spinners Down, Slime is Here!

Reading Booklet

Key Stage 2 English Reading Booklet – Set A

Contents

All the Wonderful Things   Pages 20–21

Mad Fad Memorabilia   Pages 22–24

Put the Spinners Down, Slime is Here!   Pages 25–27

All the Wonderful Things

Peter whined and complained all the way home after school. He complained about having to wear his raincoat (too tight), he complained about having to walk through puddles (too dirty), he complained about his day (too boring) but most of all, he complained about how his friends all had Pickeez and he didn't.

Pickeez were the latest craze to sweep through the school. They were small, colourful plastic characters which came with a special collector card. Everyone in Peter's class had a collection already. George had twenty AND a rare golden Pickeez. They were the best ones to get. If you came to school holding a golden Pickeez, everyone wanted to see it. Peter thought George was a spoilt show-off and walked away every time he came close.

Peter's mother listened to his complaints and sighed. She thought about the boxes and boxes of toys in his room – all the crazes and fads he'd absolutely 'had to have'. After what felt like five minutes of obsession with a set of football cards or a plastic spinner, he'd get fed up and move on to the next 'big' thing. She felt sad that Peter seemed to feel he was being badly treated simply because she refused to buy yet more little plastic toys which would surely only end up the way of all the others – either stuffed in a box, under his bed or strewn across his bedroom floor.

Once home, Peter sulked in his room until dinner time. When his mum called him down to eat, he made a lot of exaggerated sighs and huffs, slid off the bed where he had been lying and stomped down the stairs.

After a very subdued meal, Peter's mother asked him to help tidy up the dishes.

"Why can't Charlie do it?" he demanded.

"Because Charlie is only one and he can't walk yet. He'd find it very difficult to carry things to the sink!" Mum replied.

"If I do it, will you buy me some Pickeez?"

"Oh Peter, if only you'd…"

But Peter cut across her, shouting "FORGET IT!" as he slammed the dishes down and stormed back to his room.

Mum chose to ignore Peter's outburst, and cleared the dishes in silence, with only Charlie's cooing and babbling for company.

Peter found getting through the next day at school extremely hard. He felt jealous and angry whenever he saw anyone with some Pickeez in their hands. He avoided all his friends at break time as they compared and boasted about their latest Pickeez acquisitions.

Peter found a quiet spot on a bench in the corner of the yard and sat down, dejected and full of self-pity. After a few moments, he realised someone else had come to sit next to him. Looking up, he saw it was the new boy in their class. Peter felt a little ashamed that he couldn't remember the boy's name.

"Hello Peter, I'm Mohammed," said the boy.

Peter remembered his mum telling him about the newcomers to the school – some children of a refugee family who had travelled a long way, through many dangers, to safety in this country. Peter decided to ask Mohammed to his house for tea.

Once the arrangements had been made by their respective parents, the boys walked back to Peter's house together. As soon as they'd hung up their coats and peeled off their shoes, they ran upstairs to Peter's room to play. Peter threw himself down on the floor to play with his Lego. Mohammed took in the room around him, crammed with boxes of toys, bookshelves full of books and piles of computer games in dusty heaps around the room.

"What's up?" said Peter.

"You have so much stuff! What a mess!" laughed Mohammed, picking up a forgotten pile of football cards from last season which Peter had badgered and begged for. "How do you ever find anything?"

Peter looked around his room and slowly took in all the wonderful things in it. He thought about all the times he had begged and demanded things from his mother, making her feel bad if she dared to say no to him. He considered the situation his new friend was in, all the terrible things he must have seen and how he had fled his own country with little more than a small bagful of belongings.

Suddenly, Peter realised something….

MAD FAD MEMORABILIA

Fads, Crazes and Trends over Time

There have been many fads over the years, some more mad than others. From flappers and flagpole sitting in the 1920s to dance marathons and zoot suits in the 1930s, fads and crazes have always had a place in life.

From the 1950s onwards, crazes really took off with the invention of the hula hoop and later, the adoption of bellbottomed trousers and towering platform shoes, lava lamps and mysterious mood rings. The 1980s and 1990s were just as prolific with the frustration of the Rubik's Cube, the dawn of Beanie Babies and the fascination with MySpace.

More recent fads include planking, selfies and fidget spinners. It's impossible to tell what will be next. Who knows what our future fads will be?

Here, we take a whistle-stop look at fads in fashion, fads in kids' toys, and fads that are just plain crazy!

Read on to find out more about some of the more unusual fads from modern history.

Fashion

Maybe more than any other type of fad, fashions often have a short-term – but striking – impact.

Bellbottoms

Bellbottomed trousers became a fashion staple of hip and happening society in the late 1960s and early 1970s.

Bellbottoms are trousers that flare widely at the bottom. They were originally designed for the navy, with the loose bottom of the trouser ensuring that sailors could quickly remove their boots when needed.

They were usually made from denim and were incredibly popular. They were not, however, available everywhere so some creative fashion-followers adapted their own, standard jeans by cutting the leg seam and adding a triangular panel of different fabric.

When popular celebrities of the day such as Elvis Presley began to wear this style of trouser, the trend was quickly taken up by young people, who viewed them as a fashionable contrast to the straight-legged and more conservative trousers worn by the older generation.

Click here to continue

Leisure Suits

A leisure suit is a casual suit, usually associated with the suit style of the 1970s. But the introduction of a trousers-and-jacket set that was more comfortable and intended for casual occasions, or no occasion at all, actually came well before the disco era.

A 'lounge suit' can be traced back to the mid-1800s in Britain. This was basically a less-structured, more casual daytime suit, where the jacket and trousers were made from different fabrics.

The more modern leisure suit dates back to the 1920s, following the austerity of the First World War. The roaring '20s brought a much more youthful look and feel, with women in boyish 'flapper' attire and men in loose-fitting suits that were sometimes known as 'sack suits'.

In the 1950s, and with the introduction of a new clothing fabric called polyester, the leisure suit really began to take off. By the 1970s, it was the staple costume of any self-respecting disco dude, often with bellbottomed trousers, pastel colours and occasionally a pattern.

They were a short-term fashion – by the 1980s, the suits had almost entirely lost their appeal.

Toys

From a simple hoop or ball and cup in Victorian times, to high-tech virtual reality headsets today, the ways children are entertained and amused has changed enormously over the centuries.

Cabbage Patch Kids

In the 1980s, Cabbage Patch Kids became one of the hugest toy success stories of the decade. With their chubby faces, squashy arms and tiny, close-set eyes, the dolls were a dramatic departure from the run-of-the-mill sweet baby doll. The manufacturing process meant that each Cabbage Patch Kid was very slightly different from every other one.

Originally the invention of 21-year-old Xavier Roberts, a sculptor, the dolls were created as part of an art exhibit. Roberts got his assistants to present the dolls for 'adoption' rather than for sale, each doll coming with its own individual name and birth certificate. This unusual approach to marketing worked, as sales across the world sky-rocketed.

At the height of their popularity, such was demand for the dolls that shops had to hold lotteries to choose people at random who could buy them. Sales grew dramatically from $60 million in their first year to more than $600 million in 1985.

Click here to continue

Frisbees

The ever-popular Frisbee is a plastic disc, usually 20–25 cm in diameter. Players throw and catch the Frisbee, which spins through the air. Frisbees are a popular outdoor game and can commonly be seen on beaches in the summer.

The Frisbee craze hit the United States in the 1950s. Some stories suggest that the origin of the Frisbee lies with the Frisbie Baking Company in Bridgeport, Connecticut, USA, where pie pans had reportedly been thrown around by employees during their breaks, since the late 1930s.

Fred Morrison and his friend, Warren Franscioni, perfected the Frisbee in 1948 and created their company, which patented it and began Frisbee production. Prototypes were made of metal but the version developed for the public was made of plastic. As this was happening around the time of the famous Roswell incident and the UFO hysteria which subsequently followed, they called the new toy a 'Flyin-Saucer' and it was an instant and long-lasting hit.

Just Crazy!

Some fads just defy explanation! One such fad from the early twentieth century was flagpole sitting.

Flagpole Sitting

Flagpole sitting certainly comes under the heading of 'more unusual fads'. Alvin 'Shipwreck' Kelly worked as a professional stuntman in Hollywood, California, and in 1924, as a result of a dare from a friend, he attempted to sit on a flagpole. He stayed sitting on the pole for 13 hours and 13 minutes, and thereby gained the interest of the world.

Within weeks, hundreds of people were flagpole sitting. One man set a record by sitting for 12 days, then another broke the record by sitting for 21 days. The public were fascinated and huge crowds would gather to watch the latest person to have a go. In 1929, Kelly decided to reclaim the record for flagpole sitting, and in Atlantic City, New Jersey, Kelly sat on a flagpole for 49 days in front of an audience of 20,000.

By late 1929, the craze had all but died out.

Put the Spinners Down, SLIME is Here!

The next 'big thing' has arrived... and this one might stick!

Put aside the loom bands and fidget spinners: a new trend is taking over, and it probably isn't what you'd expect. SLIME has arrived, hitting schools across the globe, a sticky, gooey alternative to the play-dough we all knew as children.

Made from simple ingredients such as water, glue and food colouring, slime has quickly become so popular that many shops are beginning to sell out of the necessary ingredients.

Chloe Smith, an 11-year-old and newly-converted homemade slime addict, said, "Slime is brill! It's gooey, sticky and lots of fun to play with." Chloe has personalised her favourite slime recipe, using food colouring and even

Pupils Chloe Smith and Matilda Hilson show off the latest global craze of slime-making

little sequins for extra sparkle. She admits to spending a great deal of time and energy experimenting with ingredients to perfect her recipes but also acknowledges the mess she creates when she is concocting.

"It's fun to make but you can sometimes get it too sticky, too stretchy or too crumbly," she explained.

It would appear that there is a wealth of science behind the texture and consistency, but that in itself is not the major draw of this emerging phenomenon.

Slime can be personalised with glitter and food colouring

Matilda Hilson, a high school pupil, has been in the commercial slime business for a few months. She astutely spotted a gap in the market and now sells her slime at school, letting other pupils 'try before they buy'. This apparent altruism is, in fact, purely a marketing ploy designed to maximise sales of her product.

Amanda Hilson, Matilda's mum, at first loved the trend.

"I was enthusiastic because I was so pleased to see Matilda doing something creative instead of messing around with her phone."

"But it soon started to take over the place," she said. "I spend time every day cleaning the table and floors because everything has bits of slime on it."

It seems parents aren't the only ones opposed to slime.

Whilst Chloe said she uses slime to help her concentration levels in class, some teachers have banned it from the classroom. The logistics of managing a class who are manipulating a blob of slimy matter has proved a step too far.

"Our priority is teaching the children. Slime distracts them from the lesson," said Jason Cole, a head teacher. "The pupils need to stay focused."

Chloe argues that it actually helps her to focus. "The teachers think it's a distraction, but it lets me focus and stops me getting stressed."

There have been concerns about the safety of homemade slime, because of the use of borax, also known as sodium borate, which some children are adding to recipes. There have been reports of this ingredient causing burns to the skin. Lisa Hepplestone, a Leicester-based scientist, said the danger is over-exaggerated. "I actually let my own kids make slime and play with it," she said, "but I'd definitely advise against using borax. It's also important to keep it away from young children, as it should not be put near the mouth."

Enjoying the wave-crest of yet another obsessive kid-craze, ready-made slime manufacturers will soon be scrambling to be the most prominent brand on toy shop shelves.

This is a blank page

The Legend of Finn MacCool and the Giant's Causeway

A Ghost in Glasgow

The *Titanic*

Reading Booklet

Key Stage 2 English Reading Booklet – Set B

Contents

The Legend of Finn MacCool and the Giant's Causeway   Pages 32–34

A Ghost in Glasgow   Pages 35–36

The *Titanic*   Pages 37–39

The Legend of Finn MacCool

This is the legend of the great, 16-metre tall Irish giant, Finn MacCool, who lived with his wife, Oonagh, on the hills in County Antrim in the ancient province of Ulster in Northern Ireland.

Ulster is scenically beautiful with meandering rivers, imposing cliffs and scooped-out lakes. The area is home to many mysterious stone tombs, made of vast boulders. For centuries, the Irish have known these tombs as the 'Giants' Graves' due to the legends and stories of giants.

As legend has it, one day, a Scottish giant called Benandonner started shouting across the sea at Finn MacCool, insulting him and challenging him to a fight. Finn built a causeway from Ulster across the sea to Scotland, before urging Benandonner to travel across the causeway to fight him.

But as he saw the furious Scot coming nearer, he realised Benandonner was a great deal bigger than he had previously thought so he quickly scrambled home, where he told his wife he'd stupidly challenged Benandonner to a fight but realised he probably shouldn't have.

Finn could hear Benandonner's thunderous footsteps. When Benandonner knocked on Finn's door, Finn began to shake, so quick-thinking Oonagh wrapped him in sheets to look like a baby. She'd had an idea to trick the Scottish giant and save her husband.

and the Giant's Causeway

Oonagh then opened the door to Benandonner and told him Finn was out but that he should come inside and wait for him.

Oonagh showed Benandonner around their home, pointing out Finn's spear (a huge tree) and his shield (an enormous block of wood). Benandonner thought how big and strong Finn must be if these were his weapons.

Oonagh decided she would serve Benandonner some food. She quickly cooked a cake, and put stones inside it. When Benandonner bit it, he broke some of his teeth. She then gave him a drink, which made him woolly-headed and a little unsteady on his feet. Benandonner thought how tough Finn must be if this was what he ate and drank.

Then Oonagh said to Benandonner, "Would you like to meet the baby?" and pointed to the huge 'baby'. When Benandonner saw the size of the 'baby', he thought how big Finn MacCool must be if his baby was so huge.

He dashed outside to get some fresh air and clear his head.

Oonagh showed Benandonner the gardens.
"Finn plays catch with these rocks," she said, pointing at some enormous boulders. Benandonner tried to lift a boulder, but it was so hefty he dropped it. He hurt himself a little but luckily he was a tough giant. However, he had realised that he might be out of his depth, so he made to leave hastily.

As soon as Benandonner had left, Finn grabbed a huge chunk of earth out of the ground to hurl at the retreating Scotsman. The hole in the ground became Lough Neagh. The chunk of earth he threw landed in the middle of the sea, becoming the Isle of Man.

As he fled, Benandonner ripped up the causeway, ensuring that Finn MacCool could not chase him back to Scotland.

A Ghost in Glasgow

It was mid-July, 1991, and we were in the midst of a long, warm Scottish summer. It was a balmy evening in our hometown of Glasgow. I was a young boy of 10 and my brother had just turned 13 and we lived with our parents in a rough street, in a poor part of town. From the upstairs back windows of our little terraced house we could see the cramped streets, with railway lines and the St Rollox Chemical Works beyond.

It had been another warm, sunny day and from our bedroom we could hear the shouts of other kids outside playing, laughing and mocking each other. Our old metal beds lined the far wall of the room, sitting on shabby carpet, and the cheap blankets and old furniture did nothing to brighten up the room. The ancient chest of drawers with the old-fashioned engravings and darkened metal handles had been handed down through the family for decades until it landed with us. I never liked it; there was something sinister about the dark wood and mothball smell.

At that moment, everything was so normal. Yet, just a moment later, my brother and I saw something that lives with us to this day and defies any explanation.

It was the school holidays and my brother and I had been out playing all day until we'd managed to get into a fight with a boy from the next street. When Dad got home from his job at the railway works, he'd told us off, shouted that we were little animals and sent us up to bed early with a clip around the ear. It was too early – and too light – to try to go to sleep. My brother and I sat side by side on the floor, talking, laughing and messing about, comparing cuts and bruises from our earlier fight. We talked about anything and everything, but made sure we kept our voices to a whisper. (If Dad heard us, we'd be in line for more punishment.)

It happened suddenly. One of the drawers of the old chest shot open with considerable force. A strange, grey, ghostly light drifted out, getting paler as it crossed the room. It drifted right past our faces, leaving a faint, musty smell and a barely noticeable breeze, then seemed to hover in the middle of the room. I think we were in shock. Neither of us said a word, but just sat as still as statues. Then my brother and I looked at each other in pure fear and shuffled quickly under the bed.

"What was that?" I whispered nervously when I was sure it had vanished. I hoped my brother would be able to explain it, to have a logical reason for the appearance of it, to laugh at me for being pathetic. But he could not and did not. We were rigid with shock. Of course, we'd told each other ghost stories before, each trying to frighten the other, but we'd never actually seen one.

We watched as dusk settled and listened as the sounds of kids playing out gradually faded. Eventually we fell asleep, huddled together under the bed.

When we awoke next morning, to the early chirps of the birds and the promise of another glorious summer's day, it was as if nothing had happened. We bravely checked behind the curtains and in the chest of drawers, without finding a hint or trace of what had happened. Had it not been for each of us reassuring the other that we must have imagined something – a shadow perhaps, or the bedclothes falling off the bed – I don't think I would ever have been able to sleep in that bedroom again.

The *Titanic*

Shipping in the early 20th Century

The luxury steamship RMS *Titanic* was conceived as a result of intense competition between the shipping lines in the early 20th century. Cunard and the White Star Line were striving to outdo each other and earn the title of premier shipping line. In March 1909, two years after Cunard's *Mauretania* ship began service, work began on the *Titanic* at a shipyard in Belfast.

Titanic's Fate

The *Titanic* sank during her maiden voyage in the early hours of April 15, 1912. She was just off the coast of Newfoundland in the North Atlantic when she hit an iceberg. Of the 2,223 passengers and crew on board, more than 1,500 – over half – lost their lives.

The Building of the *Titanic*

Almost a year before, on May 31, 1911, *Titanic's* gigantic hull (the largest movable man-made object in the world at the time) had slowly been moved down the slipways and into Belfast's River Lagan. More than 100,000 people attended the launching. Some said that the hull was too big, and feared the worst for the ship. The hull was towed to a huge fitting out dock, where thousands of workers spent the next year building her decks and completing their fittings to the highest possible standard.

Passengers

Passengers included high-ranking officials, rich manufacturers, lords, ladies and other celebrities, including the White Star Line's managing director, J. Bruce Ismay and Thomas Andrews, the ship's chief designer.

In second class were servants of these first class passengers, plus academics and wealthy tourists. Second class on the *Titanic* was comparable to first class on other ships.

Third class held more than 700 passengers, the biggest group of passengers, some of whom had paid less than $20 to make the voyage. Third class was the main source of profit and *Titanic* offered third class passengers accommodation and facilities grander than those in third class on any other ship.

The Sinking of the *Titanic*

On April 10, 1912, the ill-fated vessel set off. The initial stages of her voyage were not completely without hindrance: a small coal fire in a bunker had to be put out. Furthermore, as she pulled out of Southampton dock, she narrowly missed a collision with another ship. Some superstitious *Titanic* experts claim this is the worst kind of omen for a ship's maiden voyage.

The journey was uneventful for four days. There were some occasional warnings of ice from other ships, but the sea was calm and she was sailing well so there seemed to be no reason for alarm.

At about 11:30 p.m., a lookout noticed an iceberg directly ahead, so rang the warning bell and telephoned the bridge. The engines were reversed and the ship was turned hard. The *Titanic* scraped along the side of the iceberg, scattering ice on the deck.

At first, it was assumed that a collision had been avoided. However, the iceberg had gouged a 300-foot hole in the hull below the waterline.

The captain toured the damaged area but five compartments had already begun filling with water, and the bow of the fated ship was sloped downward, allowing seawater to pour from one bulkhead into the next. Calculating that the *Titanic* might remain afloat for perhaps an hour and a half, he called for help and ordered the lifeboats to be filled and lowered.

The evacuation was disorganised. When the first lifeboat was lowered to the sea, instead of holding 65 people, it held only 28. Nearly every lifeboat was launched in this way, some with only a handful of passengers. There were just 16 boats in total, plus four collapsible boats, which could only accommodate a total of 1,178 people. The *Titanic* was carrying her full capacity of 2,223 passengers and crew. While hugely inadequate by today's standards, *Titanic* actually had more lifeboats than were required by law.

Women and children boarded the boats first; only when there were no women or children nearby were men permitted aboard. But many of the victims were in fact women and children, due to disorganised procedures that did not manage to get them to the boats.

First class passenger Molly Brown had been helping people into lifeboats when she was made to get into the last one. She implored its crewmen to turn back for survivors, but they refused, for fear the boat would be overturned by desperate survivors struggling in the sea.

Thomas Andrews was witnessed in the first class smoking room, staring vacantly at a painting. The wealthiest passenger on board, John Jacob Astor IV placed his wife into a lifeboat and, pronouncing that she was pregnant, asked to go with her; his request was refused.

At 2:20 a.m. on April 15th, almost three hours after hitting the iceberg, *Titanic*, almost completely vertical and with many of her lights still shining brightly, finally plunged beneath the ocean.

The ship, *Carpathia*, had received *Titanic's* distress call at midnight and evaded icebergs through the night to round up the lifeboats. Despite this rescue effort, only 701 survivors were found.

Titanic's Legacy

Whilst the sinking of the *Titanic* was a terrible tragedy, it is also linked with stories of selflessness, love and heroism. Despite the many technical and safety questions raised, *Titanic's* demise is an example of the power of nature and mankind's over-reliance on technology. The ship's makers believed they had constructed an unsinkable ship that could not be conquered by nature, but the tragedy highlighted that humans cannot defeat nature.

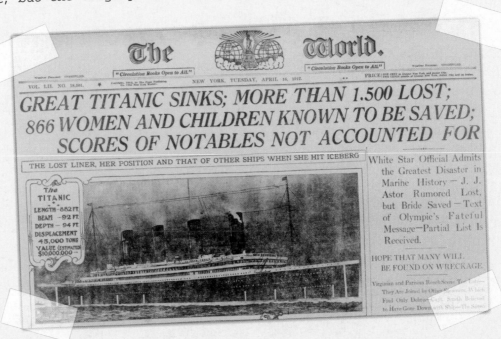

This is a blank page

English reading

Set A: Reading answer booklet

Name						
School						
Date of Birth	Day		Month		Year	

Instructions

Questions and answers

You have **one hour** to complete this test. Read one text and answer all the questions about that text before moving on to the next text. There are three texts and three sets of test questions.

There are different types of question, which you need to answer in different ways.

Short answers

Some questions have a short answer line or answer box. You only need to write a word or a few words for your answer.

Several line answers

Some questions have a few answer lines. You need to write more words or a sentence or two for your answer.

Longer answers

Some questions have more answer lines. You need to write a longer, more detailed answer to give your opinion. You may write in full sentences.

Selected answers

Some questions require you to tick, draw lines to, or circle the correct answer.

The space provided shows you what type of answer is required. You must write your answer in the space provided.

Always read the instructions carefully so you know how to answer the question.

Marks

The numbers at the side of the page tell you the number of marks for each question.

This is a reading test, so you need to use the information in the texts to answer the questions.

When a question includes a paragraph or page reference, you should refer to that paragraph or page to help you with your answer.

1 Look at the first paragraph, beginning: *Peter whined and complained...*

What is the weather like on the walk home?

Tick **one**.

It is a hot sunny day. ☐

It is cold and icy. ☐

It is raining. ☐

There is a cool breeze. ☐

1 mark

2 *Peter thought George was a **spoilt** show-off.*

Which word is closest in meaning to *spoilt*?

Tick **one**.

indulged ☐

tempted ☐

disgraceful ☐

damaged ☐

1 mark

3 Why does Peter feel he is treated badly?

_____

_____ 1 mark

4 When they arrive home, Peter sulks in his room.

What could be his motivation for doing this?

_____ 1 mark

5 What two obsessions does Mum remember Peter having in the past?

_____

_____ 1 mark

6 *After a very subdued meal…*

What does 'a very subdued meal' mean?

_____

_____ 1 mark

7 *...strewn across his bedroom floor.*

What does the word 'strewn' tell you about the toys in Peter's room?

_____

_____
1 mark

8 How does Peter feel when Mohammed comes over to him?

_____

_____
1 mark

9 How do you think Peter's mother feels about his behaviour?

Use two examples from the text to justify your answer.

_____

_____

_____

_____
2 marks

10 *He considered the situation his new friend was in...*

What does 'considered the situation his new friend was in' mean in this sentence?

Tick **one**.

Peter was thinking about Mohammed being in his room. ☐

Peter was thinking about what toys Mohammed could give him. ☐

Peter was seeing someone else's point of view for once. ☐

Peter felt angry with Mohammed. ☐

1 mark

11 What do you think Peter will say to Mum next time he sees her?

Give a reason for your answer.

_____

_____

2 marks

12 Peter recognises that Mohammed has had a difficult and frightening time.

Who told Peter about Mohammed's situation?

_____

1 mark

13 The final sentence states, 'Suddenly, Peter realised something …'.

What do you think Peter might have realised and what do you think he might change?

_____

_____

_____

_____

2 marks

14 *When popular celebrities of the day such as Elvis Presley began to wear this style of trouser, the trend was quickly taken up by young people, who viewed them as a fashionable contrast to the straight-legged and more conservative trousers worn by the older generation.*

Find and **copy two** words from the passage above which show that bellbottoms were well-liked:

1. _____

2. _____

1 mark

15 Which major event in history ultimately led to the development of the modern leisure suit?

_____

1 mark

16 Look at the paragraph beginning: *From a simple hoop or ball...*

Find and **copy one** word or group of words from this paragraph that is closest in meaning to 'advanced'.

_____

1 mark

17 Using information from the text, put a tick in the correct box to show whether each statement is **true** or **false**.

	True	False
Bellbottomed trousers were originally designed for the army.		
Frisbees are usually 20–25 cm in diameter.		
Cabbage Patch Kids were invented in the 1890s.		
The Frisbee craze hit the United States in the 1950s.		

1 mark

18 Name two crazes and give **one** downside for each craze. Describe how these were dealt with.

1. Downside: _____

   How it was dealt with: _____

2. Downside: _____

   How it was dealt with: _____

2 marks

19 What two things did each Cabbage Patch Kid come with?

_____

_____

2 marks

20 Look at the paragraph beginning: *Originally the invention of 21-year-old Xavier Roberts...*

Find and **copy** the words which tell us that sales of Cabbage Patch Kids across the world grew enormously.

_____

1 mark

21 Look at the section about **Frisbees**.

In what year did Franscioni and Morrison perfect the Frisbee?

_____

1 mark

22 According to some stories, from which country did Frisbees originate?

_____

23 Frisbees became popular at a time when many people were fascinated with UFOs.

Give **one** word from the text which highlights how people felt about UFOs.

_____

24 Look at the section about **flagpole sitting**.

What was Kelly's record for staying on the pole?

_____

25 Put a tick in the correct box to show whether each of the following statements is a **fact** or an **opinion**.

	Fact	Opinion
Kelly's first attempt lasted 13 hours and 13 minutes.		
Alvin Kelly only did reckless things in his lifetime.		
20,000 people watched Kelly in Atlantic City.		
Flagpole sitting was the most unusual fad of the 20th century.		

26 Which of the following would be the most suitable summary of the whole text?

Tick **one**.

A brief history of crazes and fads through the decades. ☐

The life stories of those who invented the crazes. ☐

A list of crazes you should try. ☐

A story about someone who tried some crazes out. ☐

1 mark

27 Draw lines to match each section to its main content.

One has been done for you.

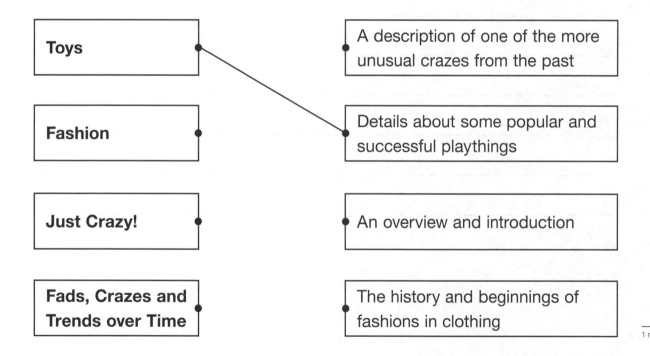

1 mark

28 Look at the paragraph beginning: *Chloe Smith, an 11-year-old and newly-converted homemade slime addict...*

What potential academic benefit could there be to this craze?

_____

_____ 1 mark

29 What makes the slime so appealing?

Give **two** reasons, using evidence from the text to support your answer.

_____

_____

_____

_____

_____

_____

_____ 3 marks

30 a) *"… you can sometimes get it too sticky, too stretchy or too crumbly,"*
she explained.

What does this sentence tell us about Chloe's experiences of making slime?

_____

_____

b) *She admits to spending a great deal of time and energy experimenting*
with ingredients to perfect her recipes but also acknowledges the mess
she creates when she is concocting.

How might Chloe's slime-making cause problems?

_____

_____

31 Look at the paragraph beginning: *Matilda Hilson, a high school pupil…*

What does this tell us about Matilda's character?

Explain **two** features of her character, using evidence from the text to support
your answer.

_____

_____

_____

_____

_____

_____

32 **Find** and **copy two** words or groups of words which show that Matilda Hilson is a good businesswoman.

1. _____

2. _____

1 mark

33 *"But it soon started to take over the place,"*

How did Amanda's attitude to slime change?

Tick **one**.

At first she hated it, but then she played with some and loved it. ☐

At first, she was frightened of it but then she made herself try it. ☐

At first she loved the idea, but then it became an issue. ☐

At first she liked it, but now she loves it. ☐

1 mark

34 Which two things does Amanda Hilson say she must clean frequently and why?

_____

_____

_____

2 marks

35 *…yet another obsessive kid-craze.*

What does this description suggest about the craze?

_____

_____

1 mark

36 *Lisa Hepplestone, a Leicester-based scientist, said the danger is over-exaggerated.*

This tells us that slime is probably…

Tick **one**.

overrated. ☐

unexciting. ☐

safe to use. ☐

potentially explosive. ☐

1 mark

37 *Enjoying the wave-crest of yet another obsessive kid-craze, ready-made slime manufacturers will soon be scrambling to be the most prominent brand on toy shop shelves.*

Choose the best words to match the description above. Circle both of your choices.

Ready-made slime

buyers	makers	sellers	users

1 mark

are scrambling to be the

cheapest	most expensive	most visible	most disgusting

1 mark

38 Tick one box in each row to show whether each statement is **true** or **false**.

	True	False
Slime can be made from glue.		
Borax is also known as sodium borate.		
Adults are all opposed to slime.		
Slime can be personalised.		

1 mark

English grammar, punctuation and spelling

Set A

Paper 1: questions

Name	
School	

Date of Birth	Day		Month		Year	

Instructions

Questions and answers

You have **45 minutes** to complete this test.

There are different types of question which you need to answer in different ways. The space for your answer shows you what type of answer is needed. You must write your answer in the space provided.

Multiple-choice answers

Some questions require you to tick, draw lines to, or circle the correct answer.

Short answers

Some questions have a line or a box. You only need to write a word, a few words or a sentence for your answer.

Read the instructions carefully so you know how to answer each question.

Marks

The numbers at the side of the page tell you the number of marks for each question.

You should work as quickly and as carefully as you can. If you finish before the end of the test, go back and check your answers.

1 Draw a line to match each word to the correct **suffix** to make an adjective.

Word
fear
read
slow

Suffix
able
ly
less

2 Draw a line to match each sentence to the correct **determiner**. Use each determiner only once.

Sentence
At the supermarket, I bought _____ peaches.
I also bought _____ avocado.
I carried all _____ shopping home.

Determiner
the
some
an

3 Circle the **object** in the sentence below.

My mother brought a snack for me after school.

4 Complete the sentence below by writing the **conjunctions** from the box in the correct places. Use each conjunction only once.

if   and   but

We should bring coats _____ umbrellas _____ the weather

looks poor, _____ we should also bring sun cream just in case!

5 Tick the option that must end with a **question mark**.

Tick **one**.

I will play with Jake at break time ☐

Shall I play with Jake today ☐

Jake and I played together ☐

I asked Jake to play with me ☐

1 mark

6 Complete the sentence with an appropriate **adverb**.

He slammed the car door _____.

1 mark

7 Which sentence uses the **colon** correctly?

Tick **one**.

I needed several ingredients some flour:
two eggs, sugar and a vanilla pod. ☐

I needed: several ingredients some flour,
two eggs, sugar and a vanilla pod. ☐

I needed several: ingredients some flour,
two eggs, sugar and a vanilla pod. ☐

I needed several ingredients: some flour,
two eggs, sugar and a vanilla pod. ☐

1 mark

8 Tick four boxes to show where the missing **inverted commas** should go.

☐ ☐ ☐ ☐

When we have finished our writing, said the teacher, we will start a new topic.

☐ ☐

1 mark

9 Insert one **comma** in the correct place in the sentence below.

Glancing   behind   her   the   girl   continued   down   the   street.

1 mark

10 Replace the underlined word or words in each sentence with the correct **pronoun**.

When the children had finished playing, <u>the children</u> _____ tidied away all the toys.

Dad was so impressed with the tidy room, <u>Dad</u> _____ gave all the children a treat.

1 mark

11 Tick one box in each row to show if the sentence is in the **present progressive** or the **past progressive tense**.

Sentence	Present progressive	Past progressive
Sara is getting excited about the birthday party.		
Sara was talking about which present to choose.		
Sara is preparing a surprise for her friend.		

1 mark

12 Which sentence uses the **hyphen** correctly?

Tick **one**.

The kind-hearted girl raised money for charity. ☐

The kind-hearted-girl raised money for charity. ☐

The kind-hearted girl raised money for-charity. ☐

The kind hearted-girl raised money for charity. ☐

1 mark

13 Which sentence shows that you are **least likely** to be able to help?

Tick **one**.

I won't be available to help. ☐

I might be available to help. ☐

I could be available to help. ☐

I will be available to help. ☐

1 mark

14 Draw a line to match each sentence to its correct **function**. Use each function only once.

Sentence	Function
What a coincidence it was	question
Did you enjoy the trip to the theatre	command
There were 20 people at the park	exclamation
Put the bags down and come inside	statement

1 mark

15 Which sentence is written in **Standard English**?

Tick **one**.

I went to my friends and done some games. ☐

I travelled to France to visit my sister. ☐

He seen them as they came up the road. ☐

They was going on their bikes. ☐

1 mark

16 Replace the underlined words in the sentences below with their **expanded** forms.

She'll _____ call round when

we've _____ eaten dinner.

I don't _____ know why.

1 mark

17 a) What is the name of the punctuation marks on either side of the words who was his best friend in the sentence below?

James met Joe (who was his best friend) in the park after school.

_____

1 mark

b) What is the name of a different punctuation mark that could be used correctly in the same place?

_____

1 mark

18 You are helping a friend to correct the punctuation in the sentence below.

Which two pieces of advice should you give to correct the **punctuation**?

"Can you lend me a pencil" asked the boy!

Tick **two**.

The sentence should end with a full stop instead of an exclamation mark. ☐

There should be a question mark after the inverted commas. ☐

There should be a comma after the word can. ☐

There should be an exclamation mark after the word asked. ☐

There should be a question mark after the word pencil. ☐

19 Which sentence uses **capital letters** correctly?

Tick **one**.

In april, my Cousin will fly from london to Rome for a Holiday. ☐

In April, my cousin will fly from London to Rome for a holiday. ☐

In April, my cousin will Fly from London to rome for a holiday. ☐

In april, my cousin will fly from London To Rome for a holiday. ☐

1 mark

20 Insert a **semi-colon** in the correct place in the sentence below.

My friends are going shopping they need new uniform for school.
1 mark

21 Circle the word in the sentence that contains an **apostrophe** for possession.

I can't seem to find Claire's phone number and I'm supposed to call her later on.

22 What does the root <u>min</u> mean in the **word family** below?

minority, **min**uscule, **min**ute

Tick **one**.

plenty	☐
small	☐
on the outside	☐
loud or noisy	☐

1 mark

23 Tick one box in each row to show whether the **commas** are used correctly or incorrectly in the sentence.

Sentence	Commas used correctly	Commas used incorrectly
We should buy some cheese, bread and a box of eggs.		
They ran all, over the field looking for their lost dog.		
My wallet, old and worn, is never very full of money.		
She looked at the clock and, realised she was late.		

1 mark

24 Circle all the **prepositions** in the sentence below.

They ran under the bridge and hid behind a large bush.

1 mark

25 Rearrange the words in the statement below to make it a **question**.
Use only the given words.
Remember to punctuate your sentence correctly.

He was talking to the police.

_____

1 mark

26 Circle the two words that show the **tense** in the sentence below.

He bit into his sandwich just as the train came into the station.

1 mark

27 Explain the purpose of the **subordinate clause** in the sentence below.

Sam would not go into the water because it was so cold.

_____

_____

1 mark

28 Circle the **conjunction** in each sentence below.

Put the kitten down before you drop her.

I hung out all the washing, although the rain clouds were darkening.

1 mark

29 Tick one box in each row to show whether the underlined clause is a **main clause** or a **subordinate clause**.

	Main clause	Subordinate clause
The light was fading <u>because it was nearly evening time.</u>		
The kettle, <u>which was brand new,</u> began to boil.		
When the clock struck twelve, <u>my tummy began to rumble.</u>		

30 a) Insert a **comma** in the sentence below to make it clear that only Joe and Kate went bowling.

Once they had asked Mum Joe and Kate went bowling.

1 mark

b) Insert commas in the sentence below to make it clear that all three went bowling.

Once they had asked Mum Joe and Kate went bowling.

1 mark

31 Circle the two **conjunctions** in the sentence below.

The puppy wagged his tail furiously, but Jack took no notice and went inside the house.

1 mark

32 Explain how the different **prefixes** change the meanings of the two sentences below.

The customer complained that the chicken was uncooked.

This means that the chicken _____

The customer complained that the chicken was overcooked.

This means that the chicken _____ 1 mark

33 Replace the underlined word or words in each sentence with the correct **possessive pronoun**.

That doll belongs to <u>my sister</u>. The doll is _____.

The car belongs to <u>them</u>. The car is _____.

The keys belong to <u>us</u>. The keys are _____. 1 mark

34 a) Write an explanation of the word **synonym**.

_____

_____ 1 mark

b) Write one word that is a **synonym** of <u>frightened</u>.

_____ 1 mark

35 Complete the sentences below, using the **simple past tense** of the verbs in the boxes.

Last Tuesday, the family (go) _____ out for a walk. They (walk)

_____ through some woods and (see) _____

lots of wildlife. 1 mark

©HarperCollins*Publishers* 2018

36 Complete the passage with **adjectives** derived from the nouns in brackets. One has been done for you.

Even though she felt (nerve) _____nervous_____ , Chloe reached

out to touch the unicorn's (beauty) _____ mane.

It was a (magic) _____ experience.

1 mark

37 Which option correctly completes the sentence below?

The person _____ responsible will be caught and punished.

Tick **one**.

whose ☐

who's ☐

which ☐

whom ☐

1 mark

38 Write a sentence using the word <u>wish</u> as a **verb**.
Do not change the word.
Remember to punctuate your sentence correctly.

_____

_____

1 mark

Write a sentence using the word <u>wish</u> as a **noun**.
Do not change the word.
Remember to punctuate your sentence correctly.

_____

_____

1 mark

39 Underline the **relative clause** in the sentence below.

The new car which is parked on our driveway is in need of a wash.

1 mark

40 Tick one box in each row to show whether the sentence is written in the **active voice** or the **passive voice**.

Sentence	Active	Passive
The chocolate bar was melted by the sun.		
The children washed the windows.		
The candles were blown out by the boy.		

1 mark

41 Circle the two **adverbs** in the sentence below.

The children were playing noisily, so I had to step outside.

1 mark

42 Rewrite the sentence below so that it is in the **active voice**.
Remember to punctuate your sentence correctly.

The prisoner was sentenced by the judge.

_____

_____

1 mark

43 Tick the option which shows how the underlined words in the sentence below are used.

The rich chocolate fudge cake was a huge success.

Tick **one**.

as a main clause ☐

as a fronted adverbial ☐

as a subordinate clause ☐

as an expanded noun phrase ☐

1 mark

44 Complete the sentence with the verb 'to be' in its **subjunctive form**.

If I _____ you, I would say yes.

1 mark

45 Explain how you know this sentence is in the **present perfect form.**

My sister has finished all of her homework.

_____

_____

1 mark

46 What punctuation would be most appropriate to replace the full stop at the end of this sentence?

How proud you've made me. ☐

1 mark

English grammar, punctuation and spelling

Set A

Paper 2: spelling

Questions and answers

You have approximately **15 minutes** to complete this test.

You will need someone to read the instructions and sentences to you. These can be found in the Contents, Instructions and Answers booklet.

Marks

Each spelling question is worth 1 mark.

Name	
School	

Date of Birth	Day		Month		Year	

Spelling task

1 There has been some kind of _____.

2 I have _____ my best friend for many years.

3 He secretly _____ the conversation.

4 Sam is the most _____ person I know.

5 He _____ fruit to vegetables.

6 I came to a startling _____.

7 I fear the house has been _____.

8 There is a huge _____ in clothes sizes.

9 We must remember to buy _____ for the holiday.

10 Even _____ I was afraid, I stood up to speak.

11 The ships were docked at the _____.

12 The _____ king was not popular among his subjects.

13 Most children have _____ education at school.

14 The _____ captivated the young children.

15 The _____ rain lasted for several hours.

16 Astronauts experience _____ in space.

17 I keep _____ where I've put my keys.

18 Keep the _____ in case you need to return it.

19 I won a prize in the _____.

20 The dog _____ attacked the new toy.

This is a blank page

English reading

Set B: Reading answer booklet

Name	
School	

Date of Birth	Day		Month		Year	

Instructions

Questions and answers

You have **one hour** to complete this test. Read one text and answer all the questions about that text before moving on to the next text. There are three texts and three sets of test questions.

There are different types of question, which you need to answer in different ways.

Short answers

Some questions have a short answer line or answer box. You only need to write a word or a few words for your answer.

Several line answers

Some questions have a few answer lines. You need to write more words or a sentence or two for your answer.

Longer answers

Some questions have more answer lines. You need to write a longer, more detailed answer to give your opinion. You may write in full sentences.

Selected answers

Some questions require you to tick, draw lines to, or circle the correct answer.

The space provided shows you what type of answer is required. You must write your answer in the space provided.

Always read the instructions carefully so you know how to answer the question.

Marks

The numbers at the side of the page tell you the number of marks for each question.

This is a reading test, so you need to use the information in the texts to answer the questions.

When a question includes a paragraph or page reference, you should refer to that paragraph or page to help you with your answer.

1 Look at the paragraph beginning: *Ulster is scenically beautiful...*

Find and **copy one** word meaning 'rocks'.

_____

1 mark

2 *... imposing cliffs and scooped-out lakes.*

Which word most closely matches the meaning of the word 'imposing'?

Tick **one**.

impressive ☐

underwhelming ☐

forceful ☐

important ☐

1 mark

3 *... meandering rivers, imposing cliffs and scooped-out lakes.*

What does this tell you about the water?

Give **two**.

1. _____

2. _____

2 marks

4 Look at the paragraph beginning: *But as he saw the furious Scot coming nearer...*

How can you tell Finn has made a mistake?

_____

_____
1 mark

5 Identify **two** things from the text that indicate that Finn realised he had made a big mistake in urging Benandonner to fight him.

_____

_____

_____
1 mark

6 Look at the paragraph beginning:

Oonagh then opened the door to Benandonner...

to the paragraph ending:

... He dashed outside to get some fresh air and clear his head.

What does this tell you about Finn's wife?

Give **two**.

1. _____

2. _____
1 mark

7 Write down three things Finn's wife does to fool the Scottish giant.

1. _____

2. _____

3. _____

3 marks

8 Which of the following words could be used to describe Finn?

Tick **one**.

Inconsolable ☐

Underpaid ☐

Overconfident ☐

Uninvolved ☐

1 mark

9 Look at the paragraph beginning: *Oonagh showed Benandonner the gardens.*

a) What did Benandonner struggle to do?

_____

1 mark

b) Why was Benandonner fortunate?

_____

1 mark

10 What body of land was allegedly formed at the end of the story?

Tick **one**.

The Giant's Causeway ☐

The Kingdom of Ulster ☐

The Isle of Man ☐

Robertstown ☐

1 mark

11 Using information from the text, tick one box in each row to show whether each statement is **true** or **false**.

	True	False
Finn felt great affection for the Scottish giant.		
Finn built the causeway to make friends with the Scottish giant.		
Finn was married.		
Finn underestimated the size of the Scottish giant.		

2 marks

12 Circle the correct option to complete each sentence below.

a) The story is set in…

summer.	autumn.

winter.	spring.

1 mark

b) The boys had been….

playing at home.	practising their guitars.

playing with another boy.	fighting with another boy.

1 mark

c) Their father…

fed them their dinner, made them wash up and sent them outside.	read them a story, gave them milk and gave them a bath.

told them off, gave them a clip around the ear and sent them to bed.	made them a drink, gave them a biscuit and told them to go to bed.

1 mark

d) The next morning they…

loudly told their story.	nervously checked the bed.

bravely checked the chest of drawers.	quietly said a prayer.

1 mark

13 Read the paragraph beginning: *It was the school holidays…*

How do you know it is not the boys' usual bedtime?

_____

1 mark

14 *If Dad heard us, we'd be in line for more punishment.*

Explain what this suggests about what the boys know of Dad's personality or character.

_____

_____

2 marks

15 What evidence tells us that the siblings were actually quite close?

Tick **two**.

The boys had to share a bedroom. ☐

The boys sat side by side and chatted. ☐

The boys huddled together when they saw the ghost. ☐

The boys had the same bed. ☐

The boys kept their voices down. ☐

1 mark

16 a) What evidence is there to suggest that the boys were absolutely terrified by what they saw? Give **two** points.

_____

_____ 2 marks

b) What evidence is there to show that the boys tried to dismiss what they had seen?

_____

_____ 1 mark

17 What evidence is there in the text that this is not a wealthy family?

Give **two** examples.

1. _____

2. _____ 2 marks

18 What inspired the size and scale of the *Titanic*?

_____
1 mark

19 Why did it take almost a year from the launch of the *Titanic's* hull to her maiden voyage?

_____

_____
1 mark

20 Where did the *Titanic* sink?

_____
1 mark

21 Do you think the White Star Line learned any lessons from what happened to the *Titanic*?

Tick **one**.

Yes ☐

No ☐

Explain your choice fully, using evidence from the text.

_____

_____

_____

_____

_____

3 marks

22 Why do you think so many people wanted to be on board the *Titanic* for her inaugural voyage?

Give at least two points and explain them fully, referring to the text in your answer.

_____

_____

_____

_____

_____

_____

3 marks

23 Draw lines to match each part of the recount with the correct quotation from the text.

Before the building began	Despite the many technical and safety questions raised, *Titanic*'s demise is an example of the power of nature and mankind's over-reliance on technology.
During the building process	There were some occasional warnings of ice from other ships, but the sea was calm and she was sailing well so there seemed to be no reason for alarm.
During the voyage	The hull was towed to a huge fitting out dock, where thousands of workers spent the next year building her decks and completing the fittings to the highest possible standard.
After the tragedy	Cunard and the White Star Line were striving to outdo each other.

1 mark

24 *Third class held more than 700 passengers, the biggest group of passengers.*

Why do you think this was the case?

_____

_____

1 mark

25 According to the text, how might the servants' expectations of the ship have been exceeded?

_____

1 mark

26 Look at the paragraph beginning: *On April 10, 1912, the ill-fated vessel set off.*

Find the word, or group of words, which tells us that the beginning of the voyage was not completely straightforward.

_____

1 mark

27 a) Give **two** reasons why some may have considered the voyage ill-fated right from the beginning.

1. _____

2. _____ 1 mark

b) List **two** things that the captain did on finding the damage to the hull.

1. _____

2. _____ 1 mark

28 **Find** and **copy one** word from the paragraph beginning: *Women and children boarded the boats first...* which tells you that the procedures for evacuation were not very structured.

_____ 1 mark

29 Look at the paragraph beginning: *First class passenger Molly Brown...*

What does the word 'implored' tell you about the way Molly asked the crewmen to turn around?

_____

_____ 1 mark

30 What was the name of the richest passenger on board the *Titanic*?

_____ 1 mark

31 *The ship,* Carpathia, *had received* Titanic's *distress call at midnight and evaded icebergs through the night to round up the lifeboats.*

Give the meaning of the word 'evaded' in this sentence.

_____ 1 mark

32 What does 'humans cannot defeat nature' mean?

Tick **one**.

the winner in a nature competition ☐

conquering Mother Nature ☐

making the best of the weather ☐

unable to conquer the elements ☐

1 mark

33 Below are some summaries of different paragraphs from the text.

Number them 1–6 to show the order in which they appear in the text.

The first one has been done for you.

The aftermath	
Opposition and rivalry	1
Construction commences	
Alarm bells and damages	
Sinking of the ship	
Chaotic evacuation	

1 mark

English grammar, punctuation and spelling

Set B

Paper 1: questions

Name	
School	

Date of Birth	Day		Month		Year	

Instructions

Questions and answers

You have **45 minutes** to complete this test.

There are different types of question which you need to answer in different ways. The space for your answer shows you what type of answer is needed. You must write your answer in the space provided.

Multiple-choice answers
Some questions require you to tick, draw lines to, or circle the correct answer.

Short answers
Some questions have a line or a box. You only need to write a word, a few words or a sentence for your answer.

Read the instructions carefully so you know how to answer each question.

Marks

The numbers at the side of the page tell you the number of marks for each question.

You should work as quickly and as carefully as you can. If you finish before the end of the test, go back and check your answers.

1 Tick the sentence that must end with a **question mark**.

Tick **one**.

Why they would consider that is anyone's guess ☐

What she was doing there is unclear ☐

How he got stuck remains a secret ☐

At what point did you give up ☐

1 mark

2 Insert a **semi-colon** in the correct place in the sentence below.

Go and visit your grandmother she is expecting you.

1 mark

3 Explain the effect of replacing the underlined word with a pronoun?

Harry is arriving from Leeds on Tuesday. <u>Harry</u> is visiting his grandmother.

_____

_____

1 mark

4 The **prefix** <u>dis-</u> can be added to the word <u>lodge</u> to make the word <u>dislodge</u>.

What does the word <u>dislodge</u> mean?

Tick **one**.

To deny ☐

To force out of position ☐

To install ☐

To repair ☐

1 mark

5 Which **verb form** completes the sentence?

Whilst Fran _____ the dishes, the doorbell rang.

Tick **one**.

had washed ☐

is washing ☐

was washing ☐

has washed ☐

1 mark

6 Circle the correct **verb form** in each underlined pair to complete the sentences below.

The streamers and balloons (<u>was/were</u>) very brightly-coloured.

The first time I saw tigers and lions (<u>was/were</u>) at the zoo.

My cousins (<u>was/were</u>) excited about visiting in the holidays.

1 mark

7 Tick the option that correctly uses **commas**.

Tick **one**.

Without, hesitation Miles accepted the offer of a place at the university. ☐

Without hesitation Miles accepted, the offer of a place at the university. ☐

Without hesitation, Miles accepted the offer of a place at the university. ☐

Without hesitation Miles, accepted the offer of a place at the university. ☐

1 mark

8 Which sentence is punctuated correctly?

Tick **one**.

Noah brushed his teeth put on his pyjamas, turned out his lamp and went to sleep. ☐

Noah brushed his teeth, put on his pyjamas, turned out his lamp and went to sleep. ☐

Noah brushed his teeth, put on his pyjamas, turned out his lamp, and went to sleep. ☐

Noah brushed, his teeth put on his, pyjamas turned out his, lamp and went to sleep. ☐

1 mark

9 What is the **word class** of the underlined word in the sentence below?

I started packing and <u>quickly</u> realised my suitcase was too small.

Tick **one**.

conjunction ☐

adverb ☐

verb ☐

determiner ☐

1 mark

10 Tick one box to show the correct place for a **colon** in the sentence below.

☐   ☐   ☐

I have four best friends Tom (my brother), Sam, James and Nathan.

☐   ☐

1 mark

11 What is the **word class** of the underlined words in the sentence below?

We put <u>the</u> cutlery in <u>a</u> drawer and <u>some</u> spoons on <u>the</u> shelf.

Tick **one**.

adjectives ☐

adverbs ☐

determiners ☐

nouns ☐

1 mark

12 Which sentence is punctuated correctly?

Tick **one**.

I love going swimming – it's a great way to keep fit. ☐

I love going – swimming it's a great way – to keep fit. ☐

I love going swimming it's a great way to keep-fit. ☐

I love – going swimming it's a great way to keep fit. ☐

1 mark

13 Which sentence uses the word underline{firm} as an **adjective**?

Tick **one**.

You must stand firm. ☐

Please firm up the prices of these stamps. ☐

Ben had a firm grip on the trophy. ☐

The firm was being investigated by the police. ☐

1 mark

14 Which sentence is punctuated correctly?

Tick **one**.

The flask holds 1 litre (1000) millilitres of liquid. ☐

The flask holds (1 litre 1000 millilitres) of liquid. ☐

The flask holds 1 litre (1000 millilitres of liquid). ☐

The flask holds 1 litre (1000 millilitres) of liquid. ☐

1 mark

15 Explain the use of an **adverb** in a sentence.

_____

_____

1 mark

16 Complete the sentence with an appropriate **subordinating conjunction**.

We stopped off for a drink _____ it was a hot day.

1 mark

17 Which sentence is an **exclamation**?

Tick **one**.

How much pizza have you eaten ☐

He rather enjoyed his pizza ☐

What a lot of pizza you have eaten ☐

I said we should have pizza sometime ☐

1 mark

18 Which sentence uses the word <u>chip</u> as a **verb**?

Tick **one**.

The cup had a huge chip on one side. ☐

I asked her for a chip from her plate. ☐

My credit card uses chip and pin technology. ☐

I began to chip at the dried plaster. ☐

1 mark

19 Suggest a **preposition** to add to the sentence below.

The young child looked carefully _____ crossing the busy road.

1 mark

20 Replace the underlined word or words in the sentence below with the correct **pronouns**.

Sarah asked her parents for some pocket money but <u>her parents</u>

_____ asked <u>Sarah</u> _____ to clean out the

rabbit hutch first.

1 mark

21 Which sentence is punctuated correctly?

Tick **one**.

"The teacher asked Who owns this bag?" ☐

The teacher asked, "Who owns this bag?" ☐

The teacher asked "Who owns this bag" ☐

The teacher asked, "who owns this bag?" ☐

1 mark

22 Which sentence is the most **formal**?

We'd love to see you at the party later on. ☐

You are cordially invited to a party. ☐

We're having a party – can you come? ☐

You'd love to come to the party at our house, wouldn't you? ☐

1 mark

23 Which underlined group of words is a **subordinate clause**?

Tick **one**.

The class, <u>which is mainly boys</u>, loves science lessons. ☐

<u>The clock shows 3 o'clock</u> although it is nearly 4 o'clock. ☐

<u>Hettie</u>, who is a sweet girl, <u>has lots of friends</u>. ☐

When it's Christmas, <u>the family gets together</u>. ☐

1 mark

24 Circle the two words that are **antonyms** in the sentence below.

Despite the twins appearing to be identical, they are actually different in many ways.

1 mark

25 Tick one box in each row to show whether the **apostrophe** is used for omission or possession.

	Apostrophe for omission	Apostrophe for possession
My mother's friend is called Tina.		
We're going away tomorrow.		
The dog's collar is broken.		
She's bringing some cakes tomorrow.		

1 mark

26 Which sentence contains a **relative clause**?

Tick **one**.

The kite is flying above the beach. ☐

A girl who I know from school is coming to karate class. ☐

Andy knows where the dog food is kept. ☐

Because of the late hour, I sent everyone to bed. ☐

1 mark

27 Which sentence is a **statement**?

Tick **one**.

Are you looking forward to the trip ☐

Please put on your shoes and coat ☐

What a disaster ☐

I will pack a picnic for everyone to share ☐

1 mark

28 Insert **full stops** and **capital letters** in the passage below so it is punctuated correctly.

Jane picked up the full rubbish bag she carried it to the bin she opened the lid but an enormous split appeared in the bag there was rubbish all over the floor

1 mark

29 Insert a **pair of commas** in the correct place in the sentence below.

The team which was made up of children at my school won the match easily.

1 mark

30 Rewrite the **verbs** in the brackets to complete the sentences with the correct choice of tense.

The mice (to nibble) _____ at the corner of the box of cat food.

Josh (to speak) _____ very softly when he gave his reasons for leaving.

1 mark

31 Write a **command** which could be the first step in the instructions for brushing your teeth.

Remember to punctuate your answer correctly.

_____

_____

1 mark

32 Label each of the clauses in the sentence below as either **main (M)** or **subordinate (S)**.

As the book was so interesting, I found myself reading it often and

offered to share it with the class.

1 mark

33 Circle the **conjunction** in each sentence.

They bought new running shoes when the sale was on.

Although the weather was poor, they were determined to cross the finish line.

The race went extremely well, so they decided to sign up for another.

1 mark

34 Which two sentences contain a **preposition**?

Tick **two**.

The tortoise moved very slowly towards the lettuce. ☐

The clown juggled and made the children laugh. ☐

My cat walked carefully along the garden fence. ☐

I am planning to make a necklace this year. ☐

1 mark

35 Underline the **subject** of the sentence below.

Before leaving the house, John remembered to pick up his wallet.

1 mark

36 Write a sentence containing a **conjunction** expressing cause.

_____

_____

1 mark

37 Circle the **relative pronoun** in the sentence below.

My mother sent me an enormous fruit basket, which contained bananas,

grapes, cherries and a mango.

1 mark

38 Complete the sentence below with the **simple past tense** of the verbs in the boxes.

I (to take) _____ my car to a mechanic yesterday to have

it (to repair) _____ but I (to be) _____ not

prepared for the cost!

1 mark

39 Insert a **pair of brackets** in the correct place in the sentence below.

The most populated city in the world is Tokyo population

37,833,000 in Japan.

1 mark

40 Which one **prefix** can be added to all three words below to make their antonyms?

Write the prefix in the box.

decided

forgiving

educated

1 mark

41 Circle the two words that are **synonyms** in the passage below.

The stories written by Roald Dahl are popular with children and adults

around the world. His tales are captivating and yet sometimes a little dark.

1 mark

42 Circle the **possessive pronoun** in the passage below.

I was completely surprised that Sam didn't only eat Amara's ice cream but

ate yours as well.

1 mark

43 Which punctuation mark should be used in the place indicated by the arrow?

My friend moved away last summer his father got a new job in a different city.

Tick **one**.

comma ☐

hyphen ☐

full stop ☐

semi-colon ☐

1 mark

44 Complete each sentence below with a word formed from the **root word** care.

He _____ dropped litter all over the park.

He was always _____ for stray animals he found in the village.

1 mark

45 Complete the sentence below with a noun formed from the **verb** enjoy.

She always found badminton to be a source of great _____.

1 mark

46 Insert two **hyphens** in the correct places in the sentence below.

On the way home, I could tell the children were over tired, which they

demonstrated in a very bad tempered way.

47 Rewrite the sentence below in the **active** voice.
Remember to punctuate your answer correctly.

The exhausted children were put to bed by the babysitter.

_____

_____

1 mark

48 Rewrite the underlined verbs in the sentence below so that they are in the **present progressive** form.

Judy <u>bakes</u> _____ cakes. She <u>hopes</u> _____

to sell them to her friends on Monday.

1 mark

49 Write a **noun phrase** containing at least three words to complete the sentence below.
Remember to punctuate your answer correctly.

_____ was working hard in the garden.

1 mark

50 Circle the **adverb** in the sentence below.

You should think hard about your options before making such an

untimely intervention.

1 mark

Key Stage 2

English grammar, punctuation and spelling

Set B
Paper 2: spelling

Questions and answers

You have approximately **15 minutes** to complete this test.

You will need someone to read the instructions and sentences to you. These can be found in the Contents, Instructions and Answers booklet.

Marks

Each spelling question is worth 1 mark.

Name	
School	

Date of Birth	Day		Month		Year	

Spelling task

1 They played _____ together for hours.

2 I _____ a cold that lasted for a week.

3 Trade with other countries brings jobs and wealth to our _____.

4 It is _____ to me when you are lying.

5 She put a great deal of work into her _____.

6 They found the stories of her adventures quite _____.

7 The new way of organising the paperwork is

quite _____.

8 I know how to dial 999 in the event of an _____.

9 He demonstrated real _____ for the refugees.

10 The sailor looked out at the _____ sea he had ever encountered.

11 Things were going well until she was scratched

by a _____ in the grass.

12 This is _____ the longest I have ever spent at
my desk.

13 The hotel manager advertised a _____ for
a receptionist.

14 He was a very _____ and patient parent.

15 Something is _____ him, but I'm not sure what it is.

16 I must pop into the _____ for cough medicine on the
way home.

17 My favourite stories are _____ and legends.

18 _____, everyone got on with each other all day.

19 The boys worked all morning on a _____ to the
maths problem.

20 Grandma said she is sending me a _____ for
my birthday.